100 facts

The Wild West

100 facts
The Wild West

Andrew Langley

Consultant: Richard Tames

First published as hardback in 2001 by Miles Kelly Publishing Ltd
Harding's Barn, Bardfield End Green, Thaxted, Essex, CM6 3PX, UK

Copyright © Miles Kelly Publishing Ltd 2001

This edition printed 2010

2 4 6 8 10 9 7 5 3 1

Editorial Director: Belinda Gallagher
Art Director: Jo Brewer
Project Editor: Neil de Cort
Designers: Joanne Jones, Angela Ashton
Indexer, Proofreader: Lynn Bresler
Production Manager: Elizabeth Brunwin
Reprographics: Anthony Cambray, Stephan Davis, Ian Paulyn
Editions Manager: Bethan Ellish

ISBN 978-1-84810-240-8

Printed in China

British Library Cataloguing-in-Publication Data
A catalogue record for this book is available from the British Library

The publishers would like to thank Topham Picturepoint, TopFoto.co.uk
for the use of their photograph on the cover.

All artworks are from the Miles Kelly Artwork Bank

Made with paper from a sustainable forest

www.mileskelly.net
info@mileskelly.net

www.factsforprojects.com

Contents

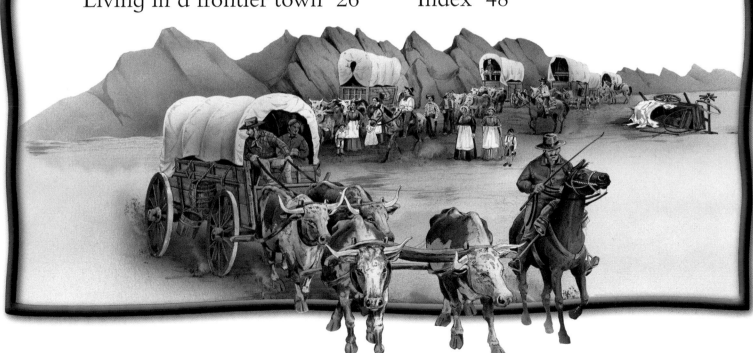

Where was the Wild West?

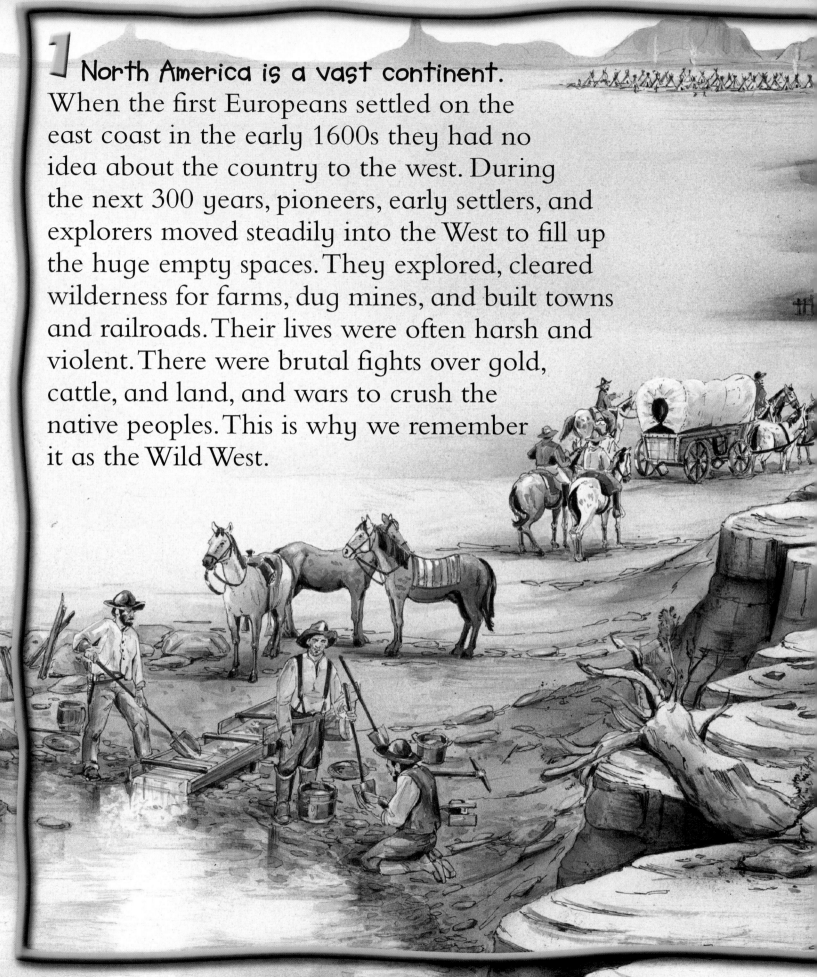

1 **North America is a vast continent.**
When the first Europeans settled on the
east coast in the early 1600s they had no
idea about the country to the west. During
the next 300 years, pioneers, early settlers, and
explorers moved steadily into the West to fill up
the huge empty spaces. They explored, cleared
wilderness for farms, dug mines, and built towns
and railroads. Their lives were often harsh and
violent. There were brutal fights over gold,
cattle, and land, and wars to crush the
native peoples. This is why we remember
it as the Wild West.

The first Americans

2 **The first American people came from Asia.** About 20,000 years ago the sea level was lower, leaving a strip of land uncovered between the two continents. People, who became known as Native Americans, crossed this land and gradually settled throughout America.

▲ The survival techniques used by Native American tribes were shaped by the areas in which they lived.

3 **Tribes (communities) living in the Northeastern woodlands were never short of food.** There were plenty of fish and animals to hunt and crops such as corn and beans grew well. They also made sugar from maple sap.

▶ The Iroquois tribe of the Northeast lived in timber houses and hunted with bows and blowpipes.

4 **Few people lived on the Plains.** The soil was hard to dig, and the only fertile land was near rivers. In summer, the Plains people hunted herds of buffalo on foot.

◀ Men of the Plains tribes followed the huge herds of buffalo. In fall they went back home to harvest their crops.

5 **Life was simple for Native Americans of California.** They gathered wild foods, such as acorns and seeds, and needed few clothes because the climate was warm. Tribes in these areas rarely went to war with each other.

▲ A summer shelter built by the Hupa people of California on the Pacific Coast.

◄ The Hopi dressed in simple skirts made of leather or woven grasses.

I DON'T BELIEVE IT!
The Flathead people really had flattened heads! Mothers bound boards to their babies' heads to squash them down!

6 **The Southwest is a vast dry region of America.** Native Americans, such as the Hopi, grew crops along the rivers. Corn was so important to them that they worshipped it as a god. The Pueblo people of this region built homes of mud and rock called "Adobe" houses.

Buffalo chasers

7 The introduction of horses changed the Plains peoples' lives forever. Spanish settlers brought horses from Europe in 1492. Horses meant that the Native Americans could hunt and kill buffalo much more easily. Buffalo meat became their main food, and they made tents and clothing from buffalo skins.

8 A successful warrior would become powerful and famous. However, the Plains people thought it was braver to touch an enemy and get away than to kill them. Doing this was known as "counting coup."

9 The Plains people spoke to each other in sign language. As tribes moved in, they brought different languages. This meant that the best way to put across a message was to use gestures and hand movements.

▼ Buffalo hunters stayed on the move, following the herds across the Plains. They went from camp to camp, where they lived in large tents called tepees. They carried their possessions on simple horse–drawn trailers called travois.

FIND OUT YOUR NATIVE AMERICAN NAME

Some Plains people took their names from things that had happened to them. One Sioux woman was called "The-One-Who-Speaks-Once," and a chief was called "Young-Man-Afraid-Of-His-Horses." What do you think you or your friends would be called?

▲ The frame of a tepee was made of poles, arranged in a cone shape. Buffalo skin was stretched over the poles and pegged to the ground. At the top was a hole with a flap that could be opened to let out smoke from the cooking fire inside.

A new world

10 In 1607 around 100 British people arrived in the area we now call Virginia. They founded the first permanent white settlement, and others soon followed. Europeans called America the New World and Europe was called the Old World.

11 Without help from the Native Americans, the early settlers might have starved. They were taught how to grow crops such as maize and potatoes, how to find water, and how to travel by canoe. In return Europeans brought horses, cattle, and metal tools over to the New World.

▲ Once the Native Americans learned to trust the newcomers, the two people were able to exchange goods with each other.

▶ Daniel Boone with his long rifle and hunting dog.

12 The earliest white explorers were hunters and trappers. Men such as Daniel Boone wandered deep into unknown and unspoilt territory in search of deer and other game. Boone loved roaming alone in the wilds of Kentucky. He told his family "Heaven is a Kentucky of a place!"

13

To reach further west, the settlers had to find a route through the Appalachian Mountains. No one succeeded until 1775 when Daniel Boone led a party through the Cumberland Gap. The track they used became known as the Wilderness Road.

14

The quickest way to reach the wilderness was by river. The giant Mississippi River became a highway for settlers and goods heading for the mid-West from the Gulf of Mexico. They traveled on sailboats or on rafts called flatboats.

▼ Traders floated down the Mississippi River on a flatboat. Traders carried provisions and equipment up and down the river to trade with the settlers.

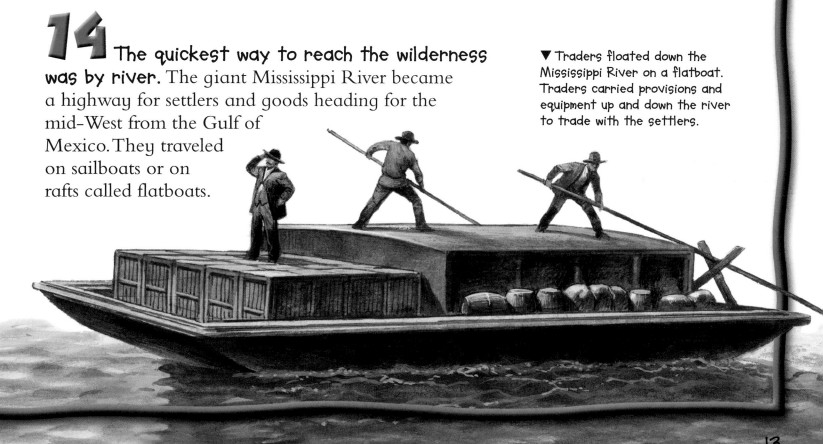

Going west

15 **The United States doubled in size in 1803!** The American president, Thomas Jefferson, bought a massive area of land called Louisiana from the French. This was known as the Louisiana Purchase, and included all the land between the Mississippi and the Rocky Mountains.

▲ The Louisiana Purchase, 1803.

16 **Jefferson sent two army officers called Meriwether Lewis and William Clark to explore the new territory.** They led an expedition up the Missouri River, looking for a route to the Pacific Ocean. After finding a way through the Rockies they followed the Columbia River down to the sea and became the first people to cross the continent from coast to coast.

17 **The National Road was the first highway to the west.** It began in 1811, running from Maryland to Illinois and carried a stream of pioneers on horseback or in covered wagons. Towns and other stopping places sprang up along the road.

◀ Pioneers (explorers), resting from their journey on the National Road.

18 Native Americans saved Lewis and Clark's lives when they were starving. Members of the Nez Perce tribe had never seen white people before, but they gave the strangers dried fish and plant roots to eat. They also gave them trees to make canoes so that they could travel downriver more quickly.

I DON'T BELIEVE IT!

Lewis and Clark took with them a Native American guide called Sacagawea. One day, they met a party of fierce Shoshone warriors. By an amazing chance, the Shoshone leader turned out to be Sacagawea's brother!

19 Native Americans were pushed out to make room for the settlers. As Europeans moved west, whole tribes had to move even further west. Among these were the Cherokee tribe who lived in the Southwest. In 1838 soldiers rounded up 15,000 Cherokee and forced them to march all the way to Oklahoma. Over 4,000 of them died on what became known as "The Trail of Tears."

▲ Cold and starving, the Cherokee were driven away from their ancient homeland and on to a new site west of the Mississippi.

Mountain men

20 The first white people to explore the Rocky Mountains were the trappers. These tough and cunning men spent up to two years alone in the wilds, hunting beavers and other animals for their valuable fur. These "mountain men" got to know the vast region better than anyone else.

◄ A wild mountain man from the Rockies.

21 The most famous of all the mountain men was Jim Bridger. At the age of 18, he began working as a trapper in the Rockies. He was probably the first white person to see the Great Salt Lake and the wonders of Yellowstone. Bridger spent 40 years in the mountains, and later became a scout for the U.S. Army.

Jim Bridger

22 Many mountain men married Native American women. They lived lonely and dangerous lives. By marrying they gained family ties with the local tribes.

◄ A trapper with his Native American wife in a camp in the Rocky Mountains.

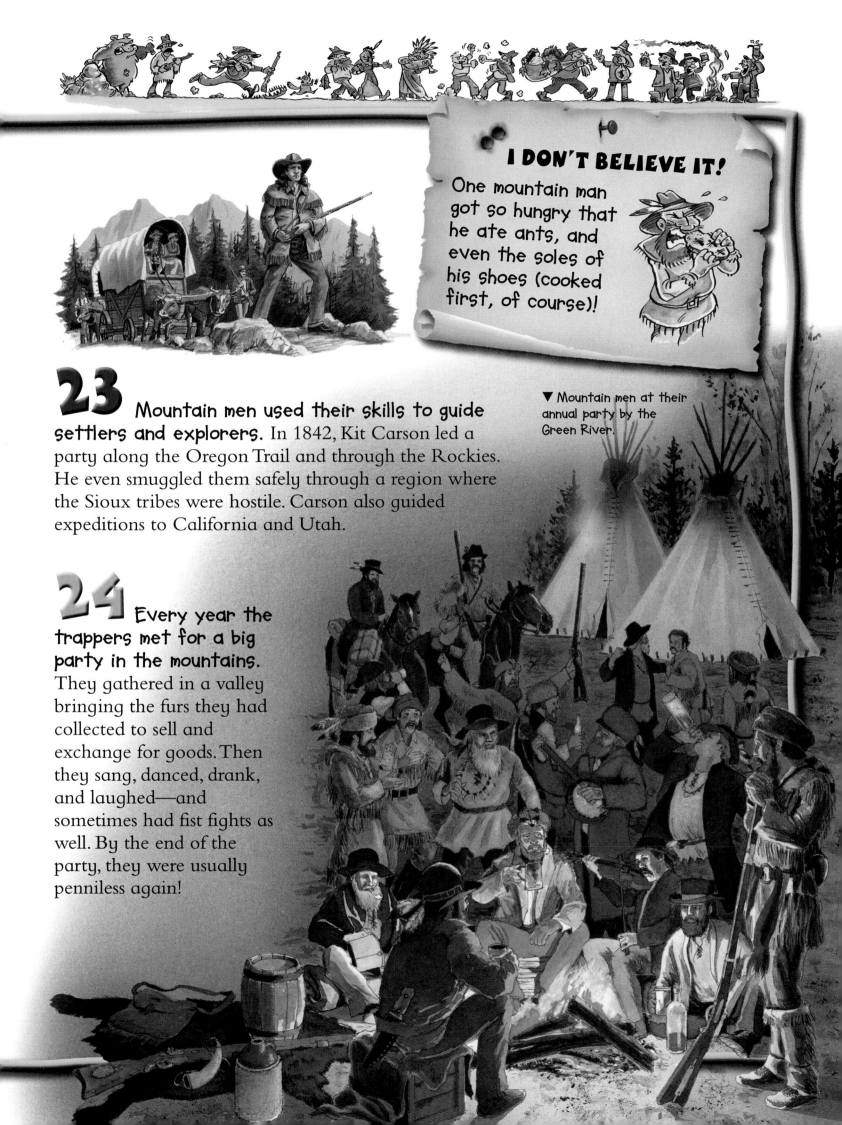

23 **Mountain men used their skills to guide settlers and explorers.** In 1842, Kit Carson led a party along the Oregon Trail and through the Rockies. He even smuggled them safely through a region where the Sioux tribes were hostile. Carson also guided expeditions to California and Utah.

▼ Mountain men at their annual party by the Green River.

24 **Every year the trappers met for a big party in the mountains.** They gathered in a valley bringing the furs they had collected to sell and exchange for goods. Then they sang, danced, drank, and laughed—and sometimes had fist fights as well. By the end of the party, they were usually penniless again!

Gold rush!

25 **In 1848, one of John Sutter's workers found a gold nugget.** He was digging on Sutter's farm in California when he saw something shining. "It made my heart thump," he said, "for I was certain it was gold." Then he spotted another piece... and another. He rode off to tell his boss the amazing news.

26 **Soon hundreds of gold-seekers were racing to the site.** Sutter tried to keep the gold secret, but it leaked out. The famous gold rush had begun. Within months, there were over 4,000 men at work near the river. During 1849 over 80,000 more arrived walking, riding, and by steamship. They were known as the "Forty-Niners," named after the year of their journey.

▲ The great steam ships of the Mississippi took thousands of prospectors to search for gold.

27 **First of all, prospectors had to stake a claim.** This means that they chose a piece of land and hammered in a wooden stake to show it was theirs. They might build a simple hut or tent to sleep in, but most of their days were spent hard at work.

28
The simplest way of looking for gold was "panning." You put some river gravel and water in a metal dish and gently sloshed it about. The lighter pieces were washed out, leaving the gold behind—you hoped!

29
Most prospectors built a cradle. This was a large wooden box, which rocked the gravel to separate any gold from the mud and stones. It worked in the same way as panning.

HOW TO PAN

Find a place where it doesn't matter if you make a mess! Put a scoop of garden soil in a shallow bowl and mix in water until it's sloshy. Now move the bowl in a circle with both hands, letting a little slop over the sides. You'll find the last bits left are the heaviest. If you're lucky they may even be gold!

30
Towns shot up around the main gold sites. They were often wild and lawless places, with robberies and fights. But few gold rush towns lasted very long. Most miners found no gold at all and soon gave up their search.

Across the Plains

31 The cheapest way of reaching the West was by wagon train. It was also the hardest. The westward trails led over the Plains, which were often deserts with no trees for shelter and no water. There were mountain passes to squeeze through and deep rivers to cross. And there was often the danger of attacks by Native Americans, who could be hostile.

32 Most pioneer families traveled in covered wagons. These were called prairie schooners. A schooner is a type of boat, and the white canvas tops of the prairie schooners looked like sails. The big wheels had broad rims to stop them getting bogged down in mud. The wagons were pulled by teams of horses or oxen.

33 The wagons traveled in a long line. Dozens of families might join together to form a wagon train. The train would cover about 15 miles a day and only stopped at nightfall. Any wagon that broke down was left behind. The travelers had to hurry so that they could cross the mountains before winter snows came.

PICTURE PUZZLE

Can you find the quickest way to get across the Plains and through the mountains? Try to avoid as many dangers as you can.

Barons of beef

34 **Texas and the Great Plains were turned into one giant cattle range.** As government troops defeated and moved the local tribes, the ranchers (cattle farmers) came to take their place. They raised huge herds of cattle, guarding them on horseback as they wandered over the open grasslands.

35 **Spaniards brought the first cattle to America in 1521.** Over the centuries, these developed into a breed called the Texas Longhorn, which was big and hardy with huge pointed horns. Longhorns survived well on the hot dry plains.

▼ Cowboys rode on horseback to round up cattle.

36 **The towns in the East needed the beef of the West.** Ranchers began to drive their herds to the newly built railroads that would take the animals east. One of the most famous routes was the Chisholm Trail, which ran from Texas to Kansas.

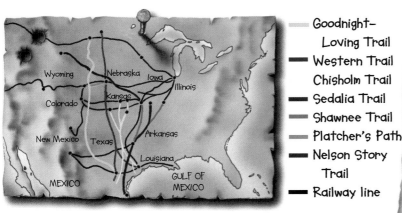

Goodnight-
Loving Trail
Western Trail
Chisholm Trail
Sedalia Trail
Shawnee Trail
Platcher's Path
Nelson Story
Trail
Railway line

▲ The locations of the most famous Wild West cattle trails.

37 **Charles Goodnight was a pioneer of the long cattle drives.** In 1866, Charles and his partner, Oliver Loving, set out to drive 2,6000 animals from Texas to Colorado, where he sold them. Shortly afterwards, Loving died in a Comanche attack, but the Goodnight-Loving trail lived on.

38 **Joseph McCoy founded a whole new town—just for cattle.** He built huge stockyards to hold cattle in the tiny settlement of Abilene, Kansas. He persuaded the railroad company to lay a new track linking his yard with the main line. Soon the cattle drovers began to visit Abilene as it was the best place to sell their cattle.

39 **A cowboy used special equipment.**
On his head he wore a wide brimmed hat to keep off sun and rain. He wore leather guards called chaps over his pants to protect his legs from thorns. Most important of all was a comfortable saddle, as he would be on horseback all day. A cowboy hardly ever carried a gun—it was heavy and got in the way so he usually left it wrapped in his bedroll when on the trail.

Hat

Chaps

40 **A cattle drive might last as long as three months.** The cowboys worked long days and sometimes into the night. Their job was to keep the cattle together and headed in the right direction. Some rode at the front and others at each side. The worst place was behind the herd, with clouds of dust and flies!

Drag rider

Flank rider

Trail boss

41 **At night, the cowboys took turns to keep watch.** They rode round the herd, looking for strays. They often sang songs to soothe the cattle.

42 A sudden noise might scare the herd and start a stampede (make the cattle race off in a panic). Cowboys tried to stop them by racing in front and waving hats or firing gunshots. This was dangerous work. Their horses might stumble and throw them to the ground where they would be trampled.

44 Every cowboy carried a rope called a lariat. This had a slip knot so that it could make a loop. Skilled men could catch a cow by throwing the loop over its head or legs.

▶ The lariat was used by cowboys to control the cows.

43 At the end of the drive was the cow town, where the herd was sold. The cowboys got their pay, put on their best clothes, and went out to have fun in the saloons and dance halls. In a day or two their wages would be all gone!

PICTURE PUZZLE

The chuck wagon carried food for the hungry cowboys. Can you see the bacon, crackers, beans, and coffee that they liked to eat?

Living in a frontier town

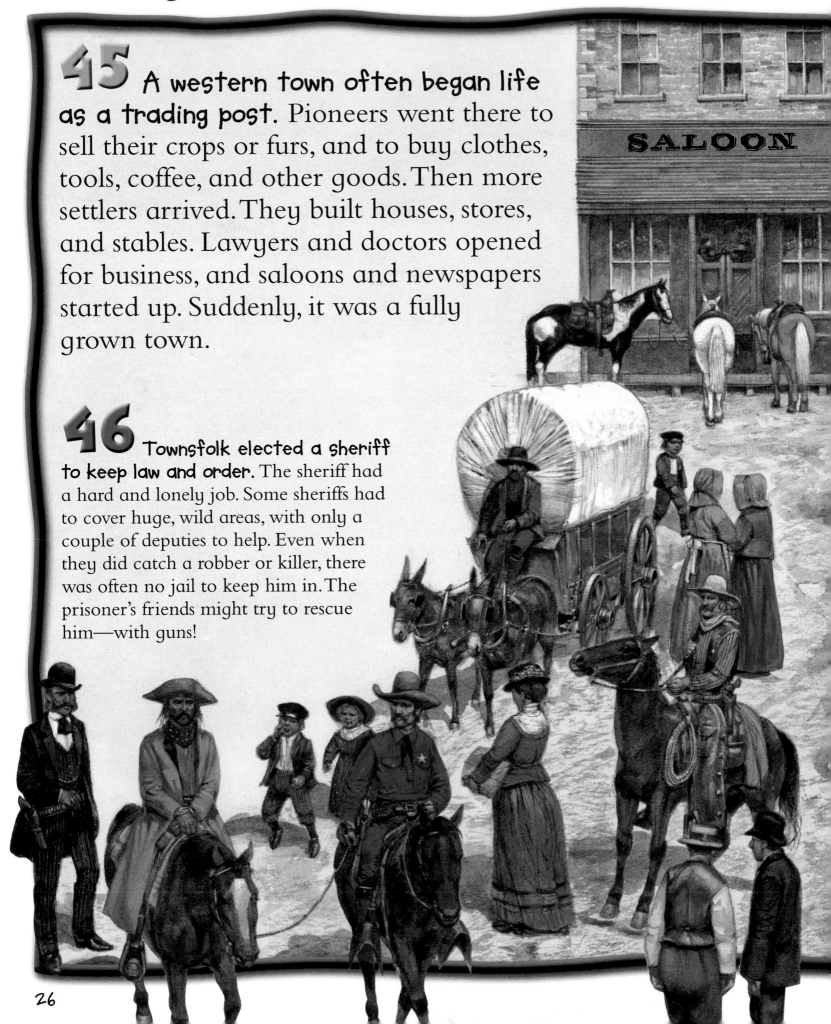

45 **A western town often began life as a trading post.** Pioneers went there to sell their crops or furs, and to buy clothes, tools, coffee, and other goods. Then more settlers arrived. They built houses, stores, and stables. Lawyers and doctors opened for business, and saloons and newspapers started up. Suddenly, it was a fully grown town.

46 **Townsfolk elected a sheriff to keep law and order.** The sheriff had a hard and lonely job. Some sheriffs had to cover huge, wild areas, with only a couple of deputies to help. Even when they did catch a robber or killer, there was often no jail to keep him in. The prisoner's friends might try to rescue him—with guns!

47 Cowboys loved drinking, gambling, and dancing. They could do all this in the town's saloons. A dancing cowboy made a weird sight, with his large spurs jingling and his revolvers flapping up and down!

PICTURE PUZZLE

There were many different kinds of horses in the Wild West. Their names sometimes described their coloring. Can you spot the following?
an albino (pale-colored coat)
a pinto (dark coat with large white splodges)
a palomino (golden coat and silvery mane and tail)
and an appaloosa (white, with brown spots)

48 Every frontier town had its cheats and con men. The most common of these was the quack doctor or "pill roller," who sold medicines that he claimed would cure every illness. These miracle drugs were usually just made of chalk or colored water.

49 One of the most lawless towns was Dodge City in Kansas. So many people were shot that a new cemetery had to be opened in 1872. It was called Boot Hill, because gunmen were buried there still wearing their boots.

Getting around

50 **For most people, the easiest way to travel was by stagecoach.** There were coach routes linking most big towns. One company ran four coaches a week between St. Louis and San Francisco. They kept moving day and night, covering about 100 miles every 24 hours. However, the trip was not much fun. The roads were bumpy and passengers ended the journey bruised and dusty.

Guard

Passengers

Broad wheels to stop the stagecoach sinking into the ground

51 **Stagecoaches were far safer than traveling alone.** Bandits or hostile Native Americans often attacked travelers in remote places. A group of well-armed passengers could defend themselves better than a lone horseman.

52

The quickest way to send mail was by pony express. A rider set off with his mailbag, riding as fast as he could, and changed to a fresh pony every 12 miles. After about 70 miles, he passed on his mail to the next rider. In this way, letters could be carried up to 200 miles in a day.

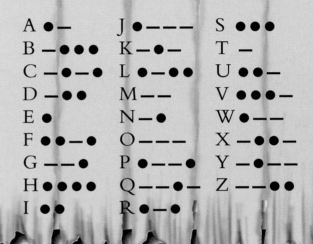

USING MORSE CODE

Here are how the letters look in Morse Code. The dashes are the long buzzes, and the dots the short ones. You can use Morse to send secret messages to a friend—as long as they've got this book too!

A	●—	J	●———	S	●●●
B	—●●●	K	—●—	T	—
C	—●—●	L	●—●●	U	●●—
D	—●●	M	——	V	●●●—
E	●	N	—●	W	●——
F	●●—●	O	———	X	—●●—
G	——●	P	●——●	Y	—●——
H	●●●●	Q	——●—	Z	——●●
I	●●	R	●—●		

53

The most famous stagecoach company was Wells Fargo. Its coaches carried passengers, goods, and mail from New York to the far West. Wells Fargo wagons also took gold and silver from western mines back to the East.

54

By the 1860s, most towns were also linked by telegraph. Messages could be sent over huge distances along wires. Words were changed into Morse Code (a system of long and short buzzes), which the operator tapped out.

▲ Stagecoaches were usually pulled by two or four horses.

The iron horse

55 During the 1860s, railroads were built in the Wild West. The government saw that railroads would attract more settlers. Soon two companies started laying new tracks— one from the East and one from the West. They would join up to form the first railroad right across North America.

▲ The railroads built in America up to 1900.

56 Building a railroad across the Rockies was very difficult. Thousands of men had to hack and blast away rock to make cuttings and build huge bridges to make the track as level as possible. They had to cope with fierce heat, snow and bitter cold. There were also raids by Native Americans, who were angry that the railroads crossed their land.

57 In 1869, the two railroads that were running across America met in the state of Utah. The rival companies raced each other over the final stretch, each laying up to 10 miles of line a day. Telegraph wires ran alongside the line to send back news of each day's total.

58

Over 11,000 Chinese workers helped to build the Central Pacific Railroad. They were tougher and more efficient than the white workers, partly because they ate healthier food. They never drank liquor or smoked, and rarely went on strike.

▼ Laborers lay wooden sleepers and metal rails through the wilderness.

I DON'T BELIEVE IT!

A ceremony was held to join the two railroads. A company boss was asked to hammer home the final gold spike. Everyone cheered as he swung— and missed!

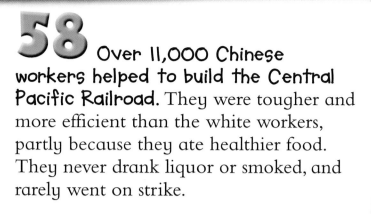

59

Train travel was faster and more comfortable than going by stagecoach. There were still dangers though. Trains might get stuck in snowdrifts, or be rocked by winds howling across the Plains. Outlaws could easily halt a train by taking out rails or blocking the track with logs. When it stopped, they climbed on board and robbed the passengers or freight cars.

▼ Trains ran on steam power and could travel faster than a galloping horse.

Buffalo shoot

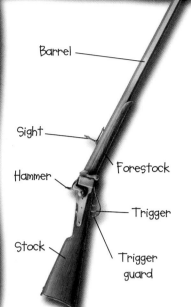

Barrel

Sight

Hammer

Forestock

Trigger

Stock

Trigger guard

60 Millions of buffalo roamed the Plains. They were an ideal source of food for the railroad builders, so sharpshooters were hired to kill buffalo every day. A new kind of rifle was invented that could hit a buffalo at over 1,600 feet. One hunter said "It shoots today and kills tomorrow."

61 The most famous buffalo killer was Buffalo Bill. Born William Cody, he worked as a scout and cowhand before joining the railroad. He was an amazing shot, bringing down a buffalo with almost every bullet he fired. In a year and a half, he killed over 4,000 animals.

Buffalo Bill

62 The native Americans were angry at the slaughter. The buffalo was a sacred animal to them, and vital to their way of life. In 1874, the Cheyenne and other tribes attacked the white hunters and drove them away. Army troops soon took revenge, defeating all the people of the southern Plains and forcing them to live in special areas called reservations.

63 Buffalo hunting soon became a sport.

Men came from all over the U.S.A. to join in the killing. Thousands of beasts were shot every day. By the 1880s the great herds had almost disappeared from the Plains.

64 At the end of the 19th century, the American buffalo was practically extinct. So many had been killed that there were almost none left. Fortuately buffalo became a protected species that could not be hunted. Today there are many buffalo living on specially fenced game reserves, as well as wild herds in some national parks.

I DON'T BELIEVE IT!

Buffalo hunting became such a famous sport that a Grand Duke came all the way from Russia for it. He missed, at point blank range, with his first 12 shots!

Custer's last stand

65 The tribes of the Plains fought to keep their traditional hunting grounds. There were many battles between gold miners and the Cheyenne in Colorado. The Cheyenne leader, Black Kettle, wanted peace. He took his people to a meeting with the army at Sand Creek in 1864. The U.S. troops attacked Black Kettle's camp and killed the people, mostly women and children.

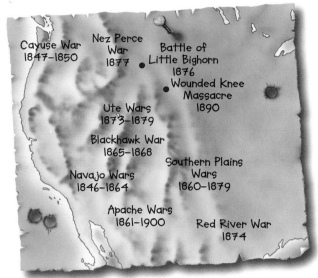

▲ This map shows the areas of warfare in the West between settlers and Native Americans.

66 The U.S. government had promised to let the Sioux live undisturbed in the Black Hills of Dakota. But in 1871 workers began building a railroad through the hills. In 1874 a gold rush brought thousands of miners into the area. The promise was forgotten.

◄ A Sioux chief in traditional dress.

▲ Red Cloud, a chief of the Lakota tribes of the Sioux.

67 The American government offered to buy the Black Hills. Spotted Tail, a Sioux chief, demanded $70 million. Red Cloud, another chief, asked for enough meat to feed the tribe for 200 years! But Little Big Man wanted war. "I will kill the first chief who speaks for selling the Black Hills!" he shouted.

68 Three long columns of soldiers rode into Dakota in 1876. Their job was to move the Sioux off their ancient hunting grounds. The troops were led by General George Crook, who had just defeated the Apache people in the south. Also in the force was George Custer, known by the Sioux as "Hard Backsides," because he would chase them all day without leaving his saddle.

69 Custer believed that he alone would destroy the Sioux. That June he led his men toward the Little Bighorn River. He was in for a shock. His army met a Sioux and Cheyenne war party, led by Crazy Horse, which surrounded them and killed every single man. It was the greatest of all the Native American victories—but it was also one of the last.

Outlaws and lawmen

"Wild Bill" Hickok

70 Abilene was a cow town, full of wild cowboys who were hard to control. In 1871 a new marshal arrived—James "Wild Bill" Hickok. He was tall and carried a pair of ivory-handled pistols in his belt. The townsfolk were terrified. Wild Bill was said to have killed ten men, and he looked, one said, "like a mad old bull." But for a few months he brought peace to Abilene.

71 Wyatt Earp tamed the gunmen of Dodge City with his long-barreled "Buntline Special" revolver. Once a famous killer rode into town looking for trouble and found Earp standing at the saloon door. He was halfway through drawing his gun when he felt the lawman's Special in his ribs. "Reckon I'll be going," he said. "Go ahead," replied Earp, "and don't come back!"

▲ The cabin tucked away in the Wyoming Hills where Butch Cassidy and other gang members hid out.

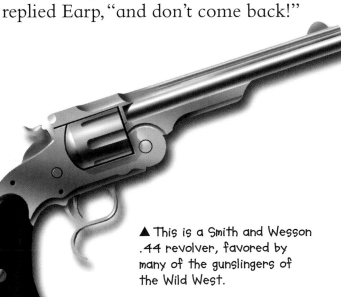

▲ This is a Smith and Wesson .44 revolver, favored by many of the gunslingers of the Wild West.

72 Butch Cassidy and the Sundance Kid were two of the best-known outlaws. They robbed banks, held up trains, and stole cattle. With marshals on their trail, they hid in a remote part of Wyoming called the Hole-in-the-Wall country. Among other thieves, they became known as the "Hole-in-the-Wall" Gang.

WORD PUZZLE

Many Wild West characters had nicknames. Can you match the nicknames to the surnames?

a. Hickok
b. Cody
c. Custer
d. Cassidy

1. Hard Backsides
2. Butch
3. Buffalo Bill
4. Wild Bill

Answers:
a) 4 b) 3 c) 1 d) 2

73 **The James Gang brought terror to the Wild West.** Brothers Jesse and Frank James were brutal thugs, who often beat up or killed their victims before robbing them. In 1882 one of the gang shot Jesse in the back of the head so that he could claim the reward money.

74 **Belle Starr was known as "The Bandit Queen."** She ran a gang in Texas that stole horses and cattle, then married a notorious rustler. Next came a spell in jail. Even when her husband was shot dead in a saloon gunfight, she carried on with her criminal career. Belle was gunned down in an ambush in 1889.

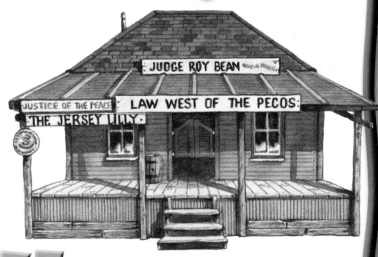

75 **Judge Roy Bean was the only lawman for 400 miles in outlaw country west of the Pecos mountains.** He ran his court from the bar of his own saloon, selling beer while he handed out instant penalties to rustlers and killers. He usually sentenced them to be hanged.

Rustlers and sharpshooters

76 **Cattle and horses were easy to steal.** The people that stole them were called rustlers. The herds roamed over the prairie and could not be guarded all the time. A band of rustlers could simply ride up to the animals and drive them away. They took them to a hideout, or "shebang," and changed their brand markings.

77 **Ranchers formed groups to deal with the rustlers.** One of the most famous groups was called Stuart's Stranglers. Led by Granville Stuart, the Stranglers tracked down rustlers throughout Montana and then hanged them. Stuart always fixed a note to each body, saying "Horse Thief" or "Cattle Thief."

▲ Posters were put up to try and catch the rustlers. The penalty was usually death.

78 **There were many feuds (quarrels) between the farmers.** Big ranchers were angry when new settlers arrived and fenced off parts of the prairie for their stock animals. Sometimes, these feuds led to what were called range wars. Rival ranchers hired armies of gunmen to fight for them.

79
Billy the Kid was one of the most famous outlaws of the Wild West. His real name may have been Henry McCarty, and he fought in a range war in New Mexico. In 1881 he was cornered and shot by Sheriff Pat Garrett. According to legend, Billy killed 27 men—the real total was probably just four!

I DON'T BELIEVE IT!
John Wesley Hardin was a feared gunfighter. But once, hunted down in a hotel, he had to run away so fast that he forgot his pants. Outside town, Hardin stole a pair from a passing cowboy.

80
Disaster struck the cattle ranchers in the winter of 1886–1887. Blizzards swept across the prairies, and snow and ice covered the grass. Hundreds of thousands of cattle died. One cowboy recalled "the first day I rode out, I never saw a live animal."

81
Barbed wire fencing was invented in 1874. It was cheap and quick to fix. Now, ranchers could fence in their cattle, as well as blocking off trails and watering holes.

Homesteaders

82 **The Homestead Act of 1862 brought a flood of new settlers to the Plains.** Under the new law, anyone who paid $10 could claim 160 acres of farmland, as long as they stayed for five years. Thousands of people came from the East to set up their own homesteads.

83 **Life was hard for the homesteader.** Water was scarce on the plains, so first of all a well needed to be dug. Then he had to plow his patch of grassland with oxen and raise crops. But these could be ruined by droughts, prairie fires, and storms, or by plagues of grasshoppers. If food got short in the harsh winter, he might have to kill and eat his faithful oxen.

84 Prairie houses had to be built out of turfs, or "sods." There were no trees for timber, so settlers dug a hole in the ground and set up thick sod walls around it. The roof was made of straw, covered with more sods, the floor of beaten earth, and the windows were made of oiled paper.

▲ Everybody in the family had to work hard to maintain their homestead. Women did the washing, cooking, and cleaning, but also helped with the crops and animals. Children did simple jobs such as feeding the chickens.

I DON'T BELIEVE IT!

The territory of Oklahoma was given away in a "land rush." One morning a bugle sounded and 100,000 settlers raced into the territory to claim land. Some rode horses, some ran—some even rode bicycles!

Disappearing tribes

85 By the 1880s, most Native Americans in the U.S.A. had been moved onto reservations in the West. This was mostly poor farm land, with no game to hunt. The tribes depended on the government to hand out food, clothing, and medicines. Many died of disease or starvation.

▼ The black areas on this map show the main reservations where Native Americans were forced to live.

86 Many of the Sioux tribes refused to go to the reservations. After their victory at the Little Bighorn, a band led by Sitting Bull fled across the northern borders and into Canada. This country was ruled by the British, who let the newcomers live freely. U.S. troops did not dare go in and capture Sitting Bull.

▼ Traditional costume was a source of great pride to Native Americans.

▼ Dressed in white people's clothes they felt humiliated.

87 Social workers and clergymen tried to change the Native Americans' way of life. They thought they should forget their old traditions and copy white customs—wear European clothes, speak English, go to school, and give up their traditional tribal religions. This made many Native Americans very unhappy.

88

The Nez Perce people lived in the beautiful Wallowa Valley in Oregon. Led by Chief Joseph, they refused to move to a reservation. When soldiers came to drive them out in 1877, they decided to take refuge in faraway Canada. Chief Joseph started an amazing journey. With 800 men, women, and children he dodged all the troops sent to capture him. They trekked over 1,000 miles before resting short of the Canadian border. But here the soldiers caught up with them. Chief Joseph surrendered, saying "I will fight no more forever."

89

The government sent the Nez Perce to a marshy reservation in Oklahoma. Without their mountain air and water, a quarter of the people became sick and died. Chief Joseph never went home again. He died in 1904— some said of a broken heart.

Chief Joseph

QUIZ

1. In what year was barbed wire invented?
2. How much did 160 acres of land cost in 1862?
3. Which country ruled Canada at this time?
4. When did Chief Joseph die?

Answers:
1. 1874 2. $10 3. Britain 4. 1904

90

The Sioux leader Crazy Horse surrendered to white soldiers in 1877. He led his people out of the Black Hills and onto the reservation. The procession of warriors, women, children, and ponies stretched for more than 2 miles behind him. A few months later, Crazy Horse was arrested. When he tried to escape, he was stabbed to death.

Massacre at Wounded Knee

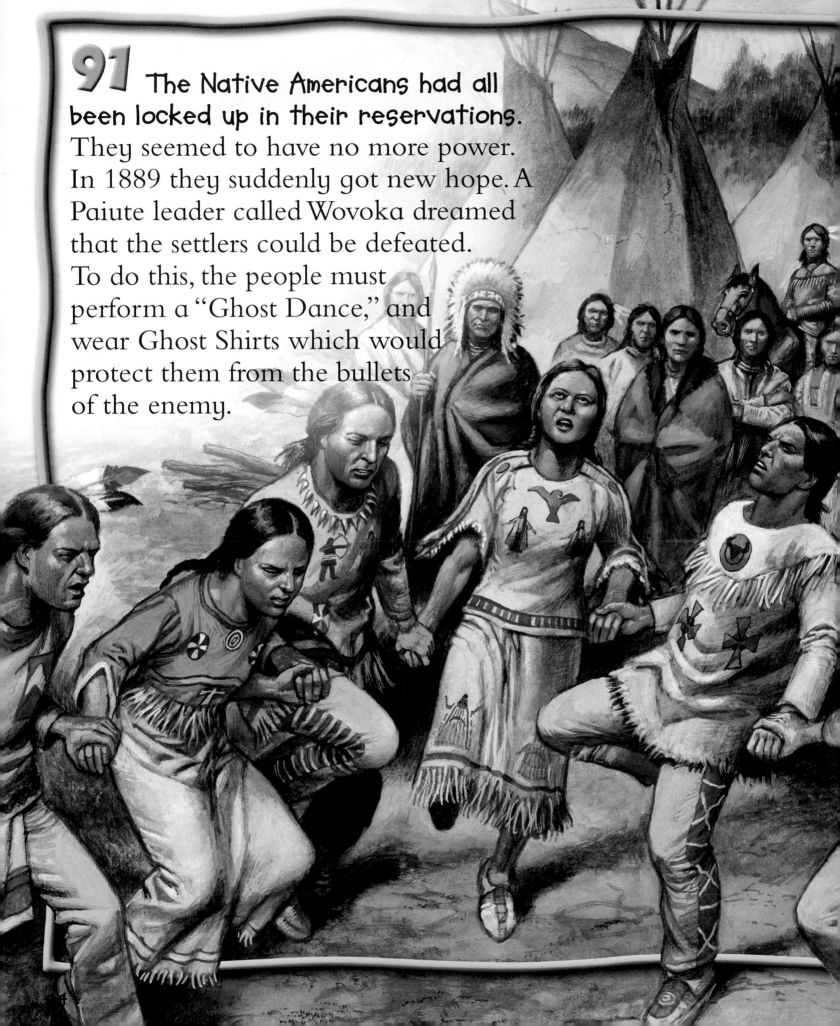

91 The Native Americans had all been locked up in their reservations. They seemed to have no more power. In 1889 they suddenly got new hope. A Paiute leader called Wovoka dreamed that the settlers could be defeated. To do this, the people must perform a "Ghost Dance," and wear Ghost Shirts which would protect them from the bullets of the enemy.

92
The Sioux began dancing the Ghost Dance. Sitting Bull had by now returned from Canada, and joined the movement. This alarmed the U.S. army, who sent soldiers to arrest him. There was a fight, and Sitting Bull—the greatest of Sioux leaders—was shot dead.

93
The Apache people had been forced to live in a hot dry area of Arizona. Many hated it, and ran away to the mountains of Mexico. Leaders such as Geronimo lived by making raids on cattle herds and small settlements, and soon a force of troops was sent after them. There was a long chase, but in the end the Apaches surrendered.

◀ Geronimo, one of the last great rebels against white rule.

94
Two years later, an Apache band escaped again. Led by Geronimo, they hid in the harsh "badlands" of New Mexico. Soldiers immediately caught up with them. But once more Geronimo disappeared with a handful of followers. He had by now become a public hero, and after he finally surrendered in 1886 he remained a celebrity.

SITTING BULL'S SONG

Here is the sad song of Sitting Bull after his surrender.

A warrior	I-ki-ci-ze
I have been	wa-on kon
Now	he wa-na he
It is all over.	na-la ye-lo
A hard time	he i-yo-ti-ye
I have.	ki-yawa-on

95
Big Foot was the last of the great Sioux chiefs. He had only about 350 followers, mostly women and children. In 1890 the army ordered them to march to Wounded Knee Creek. An argument started, and the soldiers opened fire with their powerful guns. Within a few minutes, about 250 of the Sioux people lay dead. Later, the dead were buried in a big pit.

▶ Big Foot was killed during the fighting at Wounded Knee.

The end of the Wild West

96 Buffalo Bill gave up his job as a buffalo hunter and army scout and became an entertainer instead. In 1883 he formed his "Wild West Show" which toured the world for many years. Thrilled audiences could see buffalo, real cowboys, trick shooting, horseriding, stagecoaches, and mock battles with Native Americans. Sitting Bull even appeared in the show for a short time!

▲ Some of the cowboy tricks in Buffalo Bill's show were riding a bucking bronco, rope tricks, and throwing a lasso as well as sharp shooting by Annie Oakley.

97 Annie Oakley was an amazing sharpshooter. She learned to shoot when she was just eight years old, and went on to star in Buffalo Bill's Wild West Show. In her act she shot cigarettes out of her husband's mouth, and hit a playing card tossed into the air. Sitting Bull called her "Little Sure Shot."

98
The government wanted the Native Americans to become farmers. However, land on the reservations was often poor, and few were interested in raising crops. Instead, many sold their plots of land and lived off the money. When that ran out, they had nothing.

100
In 1872 Yellowstone became the first national park in the world. This beautiful wild region contained lakes, waterfalls, mountains, and forests. By the end of the 1800s, thousands of tourists were flocking to Yellowstone every year. In 1913, cars were allowed into the park for the first time. Visitors could now experience the landscape of the Wild West.

99
The Wild West vanished long ago. The legends live on in books, TV dramas, and movies. In fact, many of the first motion pictures were set in the west, and "westerns" have been made ever since. The world shown on the big screen is a long way from the real thing—no cowboy fired so well as movie star John Wayne!

Index